Suzuki
Tonalization
by Shinichi Suzuki

© 1955 Zen-On Music Company, Ltd.
English Language Edition © 1985 Zen-On Music Company, Ltd.,
Tokyo, Japan
Sole publisher for the entire world except Japan:
Summy-Birchard Inc.
exclusively distributed by
Alfred Publishing Co., Inc.

All rights reserved   Printed in U.S.A.

ISBN 0-87487-214-6

The Suzuki name, logo and wheel device
are trademarks of Dr. Shinichi Suzuki used
under exclusive license by Summy-Birchard, Inc.

CONTENTS

Lessons from Vocal Instruction

In teaching violin, generally one does not give pupils specific exercises for beautiful tone similar to the daily vocalization exercises given to singers. I do not understand why. I maintain that the method of vocal instruction suggests a guide for violin instruction.

It might be said that those who play difficult violin concertos without beautiful tone are like those who sing difficult music without emphasis on *beauty* of tone.

There is a common belief that good tone will be acquired naturally in due course and that teaching should stress techniques of violin playing. I believe it is necessary to give pupils special instruction in how to produce good tone.

I believe that tone exercises must be added to the study of the violin. I know that the most excellent teachers always devote time to tone study in their teaching.

The establishment of such a system of tone production to guide the beginner—similar to systems used in voice production—is the object of my book *Tonalization*.

Shinichi Suzuki

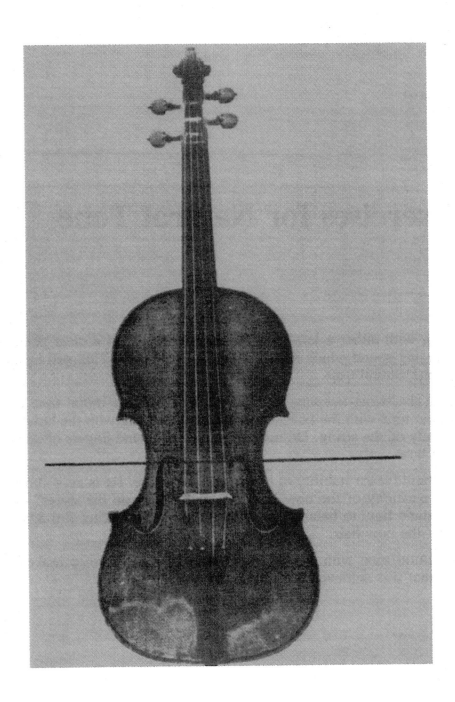

Does your bow move in a straight line as indicated in the photo above? Practice moving your bow in a straight line, parallel to the bridge.

The fundamental position of bowing is above the *f* holes, as indicated in the picture. Positions closer to the fingerboard or bridge will be learned in Chapter 5, "Various Tone Colors."

Exercises for Natural Tone

Approach

1. Pluck the string with either a left- or right-hand finger. Play a clear pizzicato and listen to the ringing sound which remains after the pizzicato. This will be called the initial tone of the natural tone.

2. Set the bow on the string keeping in mind the purity of the initial tone and try to produce a similar tone with the bow. Do not press the string with the bow; place the horsehair securely on the string. Do not stiffen the right hand fingers or add needless pressure to the bow.

3. The beginner should learn stability of bowing on the string. He is apt to bow without employing the elasticity of the bow hair. (Refer to "ship on the water" on p. 33.) Let him understand how to balance the bow on the string taking full advantage of the elasticity of the bow hair.

4. Produce the natural tone with a soft, *piano* sound (*p*). Strive to make the same ringing sound that was achieved after the pizzicato.

Since these exercises are for advanced players as well as beginners, they should be selected according to the ability of the pupil. Like vocal production exercises, they should be practiced daily.

Basic Exercises for Natural Tone

♩ = initial tone

𝅗𝅥 = resonance

arco = bow with natural tone

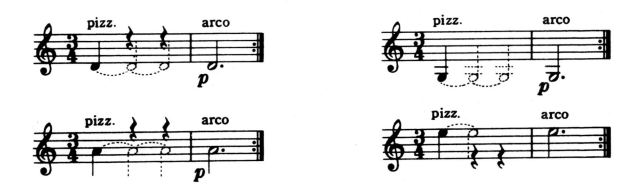

Exercises for Natural Tone

Study these exercises first using part A of the bow, then part B, and lastly part C, changing the amount of the bow according to the bow speed. The aim is to produce natural tone. It is not necessary to play with a large tone; try to produce good, pure tone like the sound left after a pizzicato.

with good and calm tone

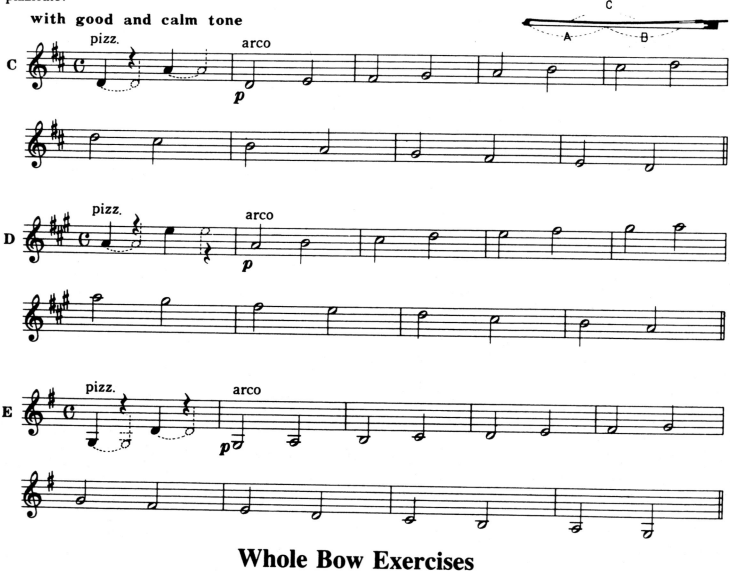

Whole Bow Exercises

Play with a whole bow. Place the finger at the resonance point where you can hear resonance on the open string (octave lower), indicated by the dotted line.

Exercises for Good, Natural Tone

10

Various Bow Speeds

To experience the differences in dynamics achieved by using different bow speeds, place the bow lightly on the string without pressing too strongly or lightly, allowing the string to ring naturally.

Exercises for Natural Tone

Use the whole bow with an equal rate of speed. The bow is drawn increasingly more slowly, *still keeping an equal rate of speed,* as the skill of the pupil improves.

No. 1

Practice with slow, whole bows.

No. 2

Practice natural tone with whole bows.

Play with parts A, B and C of the bow. A — frog of the bow
B — middle of the bow
C — tip of the bow

This is not an exercise to play notes. It is designed to make the tone beautiful.
Please work hard toward better, more beautiful tone.

Use very slow strokes, but keep strict tempo.
Play with increasingly slower bows as skill improves.

No. 3

Practice natural tone.

whole bows

No. 4

Natural tone

Play with natural tone
at the frog

Menuetto

Boccherini

15

Exercises for Various Bow Speeds

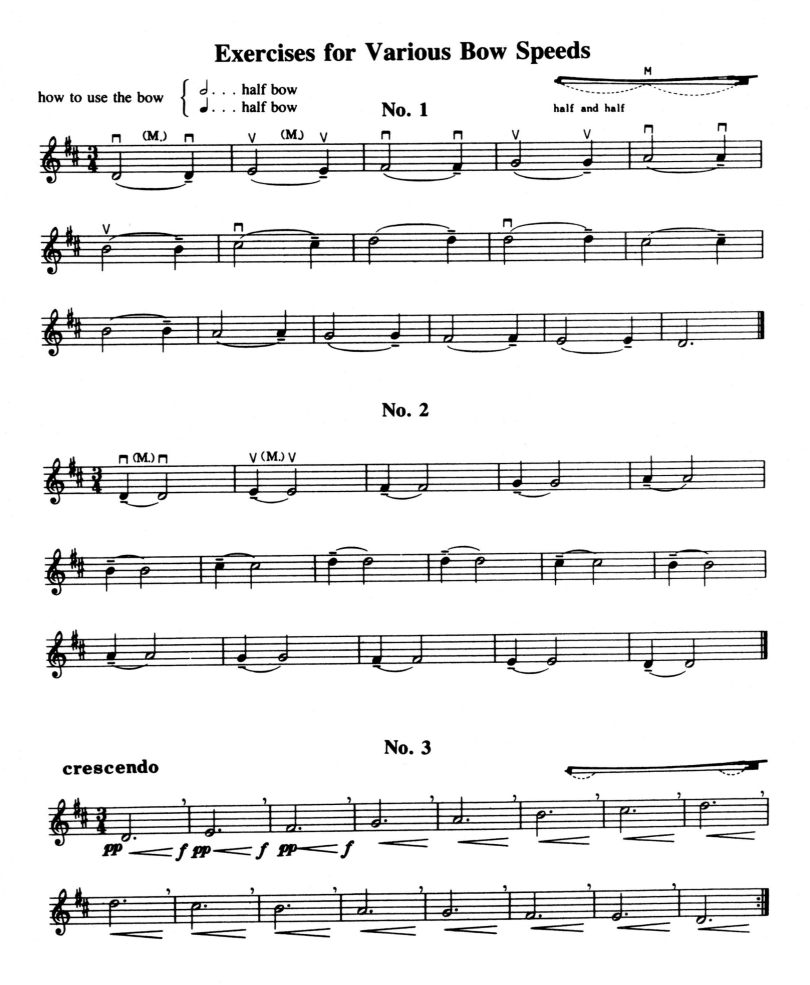

16

Twinkle, Twinkle Little Star

f . . whole bow
pp. . extremely small bow

Old Folks at Home

f . . . whole bow
pp . . . extremely small bow at the tip

Foster

Exercises for Expressing Dynamics
According to the Scale Degree
(Various Bow Speeds)

Annie Laurie

Lady John Scott

Resonance

Increasing Sensitivity of the Ear

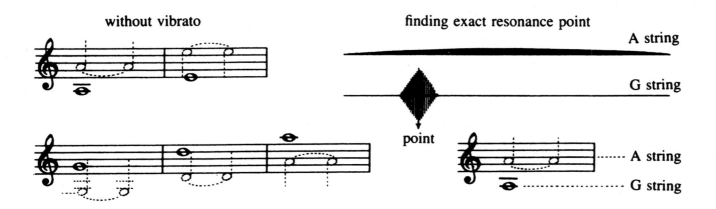

This exercise establishes exact intonation by finding the finger placement which is the most resonant with other strings.

The pitches with a vibration frequency of 218, 219, 220, 221 or 222 sound almost the same to our ears. However, when the finger is set at the point of the exact pitch, 220 cycles per second, the vibration of the resonating string will be the largest. Thus, when the finger is exactly set for A220, ≣ the vibration of the open string A440 will resonate so loudly that one will know that the finger is placed at the resonance point.

The upper picture shows the largest vibration of the A string when the first finger on the G string is set exactly at the right point.

The exercises to seek exact intonation should be repeated without vibrato.

Most pupils place fingers *near*, rather than *exactly on*, the point of resonance. When they master the resonance point, their tone will be more beautiful.

Exercises for Resonance with Other Strings

These exercises aim for exact intonation by finding the largest vibration of another string and should be played without vibrato.

After one masters locating the resonance point, locate the point first, then carefully play with vibrato.

No. 3

Theme from "New World" Symphony

See test of resonance below.

A. Dvořák

Test of Resonance

Make it a habit to practice this test of resonance before playing a piece.

Test of Resonance

Menuetto

J. S. Bach

Andantino

Fine tone requires daily exercises, just like daily vocalization.

Resonance Exercise

No. 4

24

Dreaming of Home and Mother

Exercise for resonance of the fourth finger

Moderato simplice

J. P. Ordway

Concerto in A Minor
(transposed to D Minor)

Exercise for resonance of the fourth finger

Vivaldi

Bourrée

Test of Resonance

J. S. Bach

Practice half step intonation using resonance tones as a guide.

Resonance

Half
steps

Bourrée

G. F. Handel

Allegretto

Various Pressures of the Bow

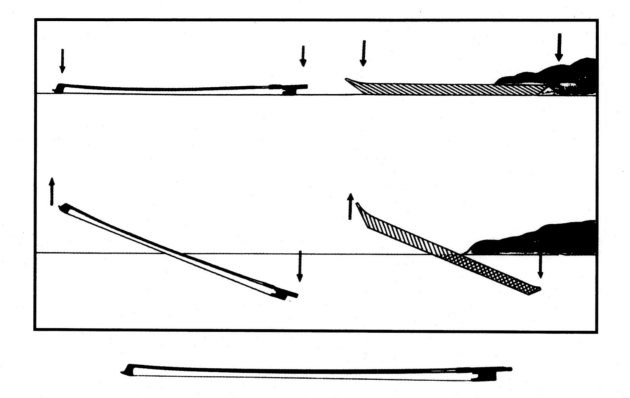

Ship on the Water—Bow on the String

Here is an interesting explanation by Mr. Shinji Nishizaki, teacher of Talent Education:

Compare a ship on the water with the bow on the string; if the ship is fully loaded, both bow and stern will sink an equal amount into the water. If one overloads the stern, balance is lost and the bow floats up in the water.

The buoyancy of a ship can be compared to the elasticity of the hair of a violin bow. Hold the bow on the string the way a ship floats on the water. Don't sink the ship! When one lets the "boat" float evenly on the string, one can make beautiful tone.

I approve of Mr. Nishizaki's comparison of the bow to a ship on the water.

Bounce Exercises to Relax Stiff Hand
(Up and Down Movement of the Elbow)

Practice bouncing the bow at the same place using the elasticity of the hair (without making a sound).

The tip and frog of the bow should remain level at all times.

Practice so that the whole right arm moves up and down with the bow. If the bow is held too tightly, it merely hits the string. Allow the bow to bounce like a rubber ball off of the string. Pupils will understand the true meaning of these exercises when the bow bounces by itself from the string with only the help of the elasticity of the hair.

The bow is first made to bounce very slowly, gradually increasing to a more rapid movement. As the rhythm becomes faster, the bow is not allowed to bounce as high as it can with a slower rhythm.

The following music provides an example for bouncing on all strings.

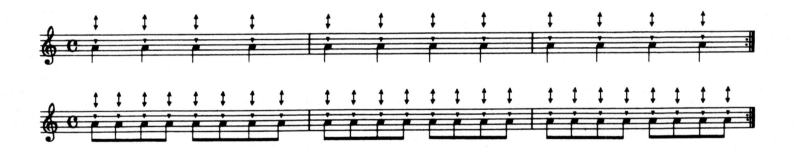

The Object of the Exercises

Pupils learn to feel the elasticity of the hair and to produce tone with both the weight of the bow and its elasticity. Pupils should practice bounce exercises daily, placing the bow lightly on the string and listening for a beautiful, ringing sound. The student must not think of playing with the stick of the bow—but must be aware of the hairs of the bow on the string.

Pupils should be taught so that the right arm can move freely up and down according to the bow movement (refer to "ship on the water").

30

Exercises for Light Spiccato

Practice until a good, firm tone is produced. A weak tone will result if the balance of the bow is not kept when the bow falls down on the string, or if the bow is held too tightly.

Various Pressures on the Strings
(Keeping the bow lightly on the string)

Exercises for Change of Bow Weight on the String

No. 2

No. 3

preparatory exercises

Menuetto in G

L. van Beethoven

Allegretto

Country Dance

Weber

Exercises for Change of Bow Weight (Pressure)
Using Elasticity of Hair

Begin and end each bow with a natural tone.

Concerto in A Minor
Largo

A. Vivaldi

Concerto in G Minor
Adagio

A. Vivaldi

Various Tone Colors

Exercises for Positioning of the Bow

The nearer the bow to the bridge, the more the overtones increase, causing greater volume.

The author of *Kreisler* says in his book that Mr. Kreisler often played near the bridge.

The following facts can be observed about the various positions of bowing indicated in the picture above:

1. The nearer the bridge, the greater the resistance of tension.
2. The nearer the bridge, the greater the overtone presence.
3. The nearer the fingerboard, the softer the tone.
4. Thus, if the bow is away from the bridge, a soft tone results.

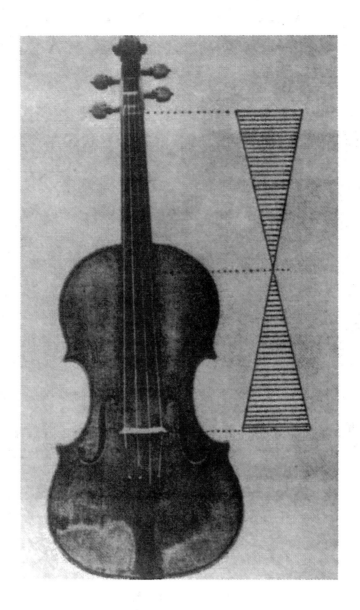

This picture shows the relationship between tone, volume and pressure in proportion to distance from the middle of the string.

1. The nearer the bridge, the greater the overtone content.

2. The nearer the bridge, the greater the pressure required, otherwise the string will not vibrate.

3. Therefore, the nearer the bridge, the greater the volume.

4. The nearer the middle of the string, the softer the tone.

5. The nearer the middle of the string, the less pressure required.

6. Pizzicato of left and right hands will be softer if played nearer to the middle of the string.

7. The nearer to the bridge, the sharper the pizzicato and the greater the overtone content.

Exercises for Playing Near the Bridge

Produce strong, fine overtones and watch the path of the bow.

Old Folks at Home

Foster

40

Concerto in G Minor
Adagio

Exercises for various tone colors

Bruch

Sonata in G Minor
Grave

Exercises for various tone colors

Henri Eccles

Exercises for various tone colors

Sonata in G Minor
Adagio

Henri Eccles

Teaching Suggestions

Vital Point to Produce the Rich Sound
of an Artist

The beautiful, rich tone of a skilled performer is produced by the horsehair, as it were, stuck fast to the string with the bow set lightly on the string.

The beginner sometimes produces a scratching and scraping sound because he cannot control the bow. When he tries to play lightly, his bow is often too loose and slippery; when he tries to play strongly, then the scratching tone occurs.

This is one of the troubles of beginners. (Refer to "ship on the water," p. 33, and "important function of forefinger and thumb," p. 52.)

Tone can be produced only with the weight of the bow set on the string. Therefore, the pupil must first master control of the bow on the string (in the beginning it is hard to set the bow on the string without pressure) and secondly, the pupil must unstiffen and free his right hand when playing.

But the beginner cannot produce good, firm tone even if he can set the bow on the string without pressure. Why is this? It is because the beginner loses the weight of the bow while drawing the bow on the string. The pupil must gain the ability to draw the bow and have it stick to the string with the help of the elasticity of the hair.

"Horsehair is Scotch tape." These exercises explain how to hold the bow, how to set the bow, and how to use the weight of the bow to keep it stuck fast to the string, just like Scotch tape.

How to Relax Stiff Fingers When Holding the Bow

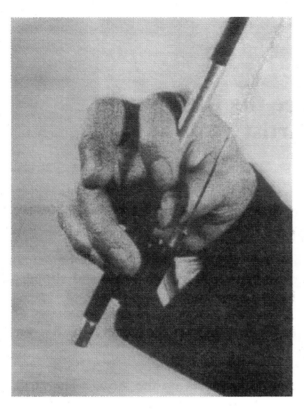 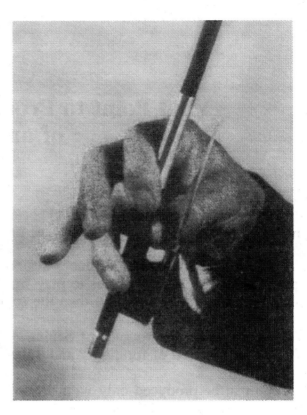

A   B

A stiff hand is caused by all five fingers holding the bow, especially the middle finger or the forefinger. I, myself, keep the middle finger idle (see above).

A with the forefinger, the ring finger and the little finger
B with the forefinger and ring finger

Pupils should practice, for example, "Perpetual Motion" or a scale, always using ♪♫ for several months, first with bow hold A, then B, and finally with the forefinger and the middle finger.

Thumb Position on the Bow

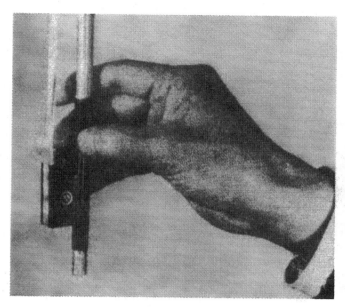 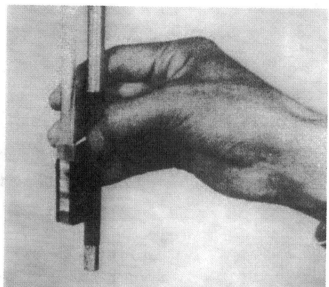

A   B

The position of the ball of the thumb on the bow should be carefully observed. Some pupils play with a twisted hand caused by placing the thumb at an improper angle.

The teacher should ask the pupil to hold the bow, rotating the thumb from left to middle to right, observing the position of the hand at all times. Ideally, as in photo B, the proper hand position is achieved when the thumb is angled so that the right side near the edge of the nail is holding the bow.

Function of the Forefinger and the Thumb

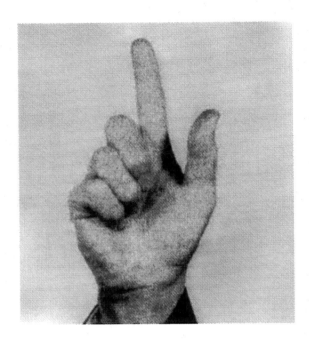

The forefinger is the most important finger in controlling the balance of the bow. However, we must not ignore the function of the thumb.

Proper holding of the bow results from the co-operation between forefinger and thumb (the balance of power on the upper and lower sides); the forefinger without the help of the thumb causes a crunching sound. Therefore, the co-operation of both is necessary for producing good tone.

How to Hold the Bow for Good Tone
Power of the Forefinger and Thumb

A soft tone is produced if we play the string with the bow held lightly. But, if we want to produce rich, clear tone, we must hold the bow more securely to control it all the way to the tip.

It is important to develop the pupil's ability to hold the bow securely with thumb, forefinger, ring finger and little finger (see photo).

When this bowhold is secure, place the bow lightly on the string and strive for clear tone. (Do not press the bow stick.) After the pupil achieves good, clear tone he should add the middle finger.

Stiffness of the Little Finger
Destroys All Balance

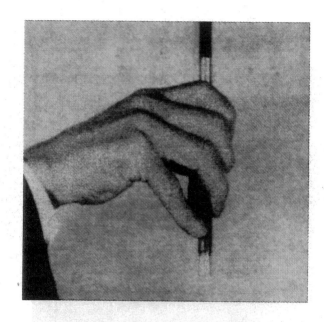

The little finger, as seen in the picture, should be freed from such stiffness as early as possible. If the little finger is stiff, the tip of the bow loses its weight and the right hand becomes stiff also.

- Twisted right hand (often caused by holding the bow at the middle of the thumb)
- Little finger pressed tightly

Pupils with these particular problems should practice holding the bow without using the little finger. It is also helpful to practice putting the thumb under the frog.

Adjustment of Drooping Scroll

A   B

The drooping scroll comes mainly from improper posture—leaning forward.

If the pupil corrects his posture but still has a drooping scroll, as in photo B, I suggest that the pupil hold the violin in such a way that the elbow of the left arm is away from the body, as in photo A. Also suggest that the distance of the elbow from the body should be great enough to allow a dish to be held between the elbow and the body.

Bowing in a Straight Line

The pupil should pull the bow in a straight line parallel to the bridge. If his bow curves, it is the result of improperly pulling the elbow to the right side of the body.

Such pupils are taught the proper bow stroke by directing the right hand to the right knee, positioned as seen in the picture.

Pupils should master the proper stroke in several months.

Holding the Bow Under the Frog

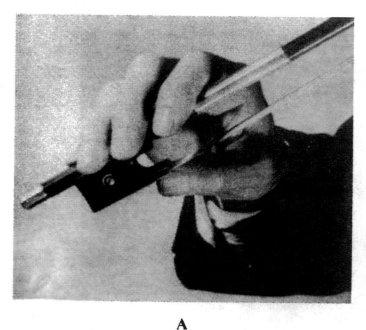

A

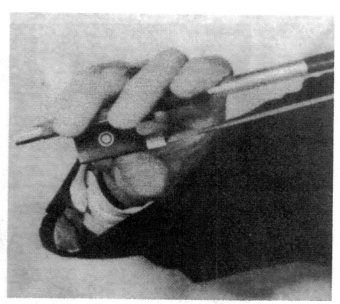

B

Beginning pupils who are unable to make good tone are likely to press the string with the bow. To avoid this habit, beginning pupils may be taught at first to hold the bow under the frog as seen in photo A. A year later, perhaps, they will be taught to hold the bow in the proper way.

Sometimes, more advanced pupils with weak tone are also instructed to play with the bow held under the frog. Photo B shows a twisted hand resulting from an improper thumb angle.

Every Child Can Be Educated

Hiromi Kiuchi, at the age of five months, recognized the first movement of the Vivaldi Concerto in G Minor.

If a newborn baby listens daily to the same piece, he will come to recognize it and be able to distinguish it from other music.

After thirty years of experience, I know that if young children listen to good music repeatedly they will develop a keen musical sense. Musical talent is not inherited!

As every child can learn to speak this native language, he can be educated in other areas if he is given the right environment.

The motto of Talent Education is "Every child can be educated."

Let's Have a Good Time
Group Lessons are Fun and Develop Ability

Children love to play music with their friends. Pupils who have the opportunity to participate in group lessons make remarkable improvement in tone quality, posture, and musicality. The presence of more advanced pupils in the group lesson helps newer pupils to learn.

All Talent Education programs provide group lessons, thus providing a happy learning experience. I believe education must be warm and pleasant.

Adjustment of the Shape of the Left Hand
Observations of its Motion

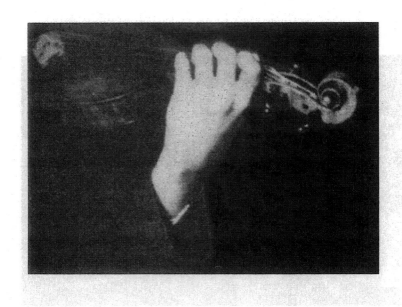

One of the teacher's responsibilities is to adjust the shape of the pupil's left hand.

I observe the shape and motion of the pupil's left hand from the angle from which this picture was taken. I make sure the shape is correct, and that the left hand moves up and down, maintaining this shape in all positions. The left hand should be adjusted as early as possible.

Our Movement and Our Hope

(Mr. Shinichi Suzuki's preface to the program presented by
1500 Japanese children in Tokyo, March 1958.)

All human beings are born with great potentialities, and each individual has within himself the capacity for developing to a very high level.

Although some individuals display a remarkable ability during their lifetime, we are not concerned here with these extraordinary cases. However, there are many others who are born with great potential who, through unfavorable conditions, fail to develop to their proper level of achievement.

Education begins from the day of birth. We must recognize the amazing power of the infant who absorbs everything in his surroundings and adds to his knowledge. If attention is not given to early infancy, how can the child's innate potential be developed? We learn from nature that a plant which is damaged or stunted during the sapling stage does not have a promising future. Yet at present, we know very little about proper training for the early infancy of human beings. Therefore, we must learn more about the conditions in which early human growth takes place.

Though still in an experimental stage, Talent Education has realized that all children in the world show their splendid capacities by speaking and understanding their mother language, thus displaying the potential of the human mind. *Is it not probable that this mother language method holds the key to human development?*

Talent Education has applied this method to the teaching of music: children, taken without previous aptitude or intelligence tests of any kind, have almost without exception made great progress.

Cultural sensitivity is not inherited, but is developed after birth. The hereditary ability of the mind is measured by the speed with which it adapts to circumstances. It is wrong to assume that special talent for learning music, literature, or any other field, is primarily inherited.

This is not to say that everyone can reach the same level of achievement. However, each individual can certainly achieve the equivalent of his language proficiency in other fields. We must investigate methods through which all children can develop their various talents. This may be more important than the investigation of atomic power. After twelve years, Talent Education now demonstrates the harvest of its educational experiment in music, and after observing and hearing the performances of these children, we adults should reflect and consider whether this method is not the best way to develop all human talents.

(Translation and digest made through collaboration of Dr. Honda,
Mr. and Mrs. David Hoshino, and Mr. Kendall.)